Samuel de Champlain

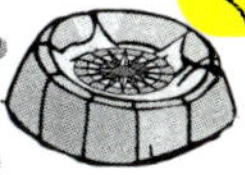

Father of New France

Samuel's father, Antoine Champlain, was a sea captain. His uncle was a geographer.

Samuel de Champlain was born at Brouage, on the Bay of Biscay in France about 1570. Samuel's parents may have been members of the lower nobility.

Solve the code to discover the name of Samuel's mother.

A	B	C	D	E	F	G	H	I	J	K	L	M

N	O	P	Q	R	S	T	U	V	W	X	Y	Z

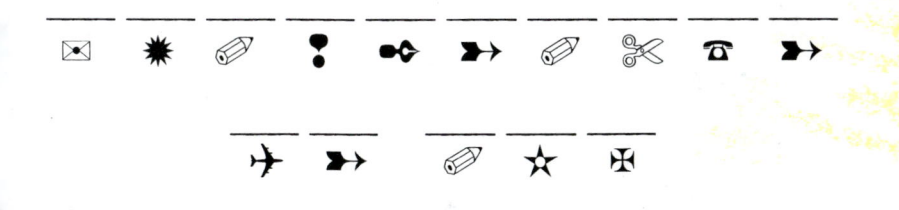

M A R G U E R I T E

L E R O Y

While Samuel was still very young, he traveled with his father and uncle on several voyages to the New World.

Samuel learned a lot from his father and uncle. He learned to be a navigator, a geographer, and a cartographer.

"Pull" apart the words to find out something about cartographers.

Acartographerissomeonewhomakesmapsorstudiesthem.

Samuel learned to read and write from the parish priest.

When Samuel was about twenty years old, he volunteered his services to the Maréchal d'Aumont, a commander for the Catholic Army. The army was fighting another group of Christians called the Huguenots.

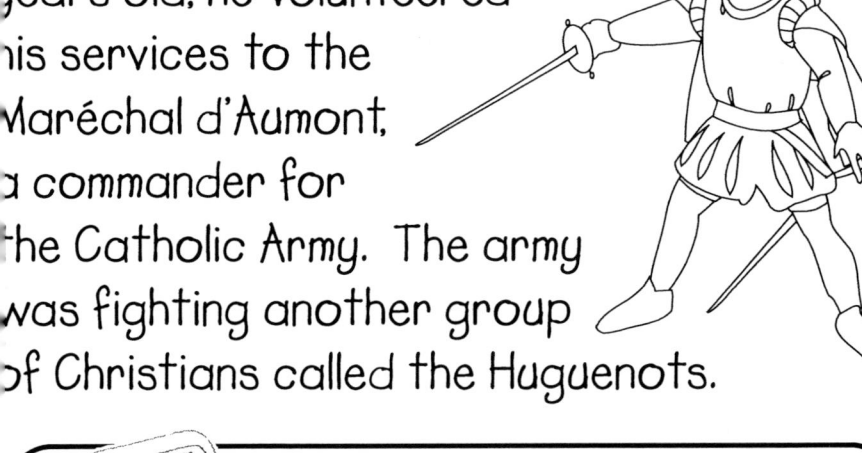

What year did Samuel volunteer for the Army?

1570 (Year Samuel was born)

+ 20 (How old he was when he volunteered)

_____ (Year Samuel volunteered)

Huguenots were a group of Protestants who quarreled with Catholics in France during the 1500s and 1600s.

Samuel did not like being a soldier. He wanted to be a navigator like his father and uncle. Samuel enjoyed exploring "new countries, regions, and realms."

Which came first?

___ Samuel volunteered for the army.

___ Samuel traveled with his father and uncle.

___ Samuel decided that he wanted to be a navigator.

Samuel wrote a book about his travels to the Gulf of Mexico. He was the first to suggest building a canal across Panama.

About 1602, King Henry IV read the book Samuel had written about his travels. The King was so impressed that he made Samuel a royal geographer.

Explorers used several tools for navigation. Match the picture of each navigational tool with its name.

Explorers used several tools for navigation.

Match the picture of each navigational tool with its name.

CHART

COMPASS

SPYGLASS

LOGBOOK

Samuel's first trip to New France (present-day Canada), was a fur-trading expedition. The Montagnais tribe brought furs to trade for French cloth and metal tools.

Samuel made a second trip to New France in 1604. Samuel continued making excellent maps of rivers all up and down the coast. Samuel tried to establish a settlement on

Find the words in the Word Find below.

MAP   RIVER   COAST

U	W	O	D
P	I	H	S
P	D	V	O
X	A	A	O
F	S	M	W
T	E	O	O
A	V	P	Q
T	R	A	D

The French named the area that Samuel explored on his second trip Acadia.

Samuel's men died of scurvy. This is a disease caused by not getting enough vitamin C.

the Atlantic Coast. Seventy-nine men stayed there during the winter of 1604 to 1605. Thirty-five of them died. Samuel stayed there for three years.

SHIP	TRADING	VOYAGE
T	R	L	U
C	I	T	G
K	V	C	V
S	E	K	O
Y	R	F	N
R	A	P	X
Q	W	G	E
I	N	G	E

Samuel hoped to find silver on his second trip to New France.

In the spring of 1605, the men moved their camp and renamed in Port Royal.

Samuel made his third trip to New France in 1608. He established the first permanent European settlement in Canada. He named the city Québec.

Samuel wanted to establish a permanent post where he could trade French goods for furs.

Unscramble the words in the sentences below to learn more about Samuel de Champlain.

Samuel wanted to _____
eorexpl

and _____ the new continent.
pam

He also wanted to _____ a route
infd

to the _____ Ocean.
ccifPai

In 1612, Samuel was given the title of lieutenant of the viceroy of New France.

Champlain made many more trips between Québec and France. In 1627, Cardinal Richelieu and others called the "Company of One Hundred Associates" gave Samuel money so that Québec would grow. They hoped to get rich by selling the New World's natural resources.

In 1610, Samuel married Hélene Boull. She travelled with Samuel to Québec in 1620. She stayed four years before returning to France!

THE LAKE NAMESAKE!

Which two states share a lake named after Champlain?
Unscramble these letters to find out:

___ ___ ___ ___ ___ ___ ___ ___
W   E   N   O   Y   R   R   K

___ ___ ___ ___ ___ ___ ___ ___
E   R   T   M   N   O   V

Samuel de Champlain died at Québec on December 25, 1635. Many of his observations were published in the large body of writing he left behind. All of his writings and maps filled up six volumes!

Color the picture of Samuel de Champlain.

Samuel governed the city of Québec until he died.

Glossary

cartographer: someone who makes maps or charts

hydrographer: someone who measures and charts seas, lakes, rivers, and other bodies of water

navigator: person in charge of position and course of a ship

natural resources: materials supplied by nature that are useful or necessary for life

Huguenots: French Protestant of the 1500s and 1600s

Pop Quiz!

1. Where was Samuel born?
   - ○ England
   - ○ Spain
   - ○ France

2. Who taught Samuel how to be a navigator?
   - ○ Mother and Father
   - ○ Father and Uncle
   - ○ Grandmother and priest

3. Which one was a group of French Protestants?
   - ○ Cosmonauts
   - ○ Huguenots
   - ○ Astronauts

4. Which city did Samuel start as a trading post?
   - ○ Montreal
   - ○ Québec
   - ○ Ottawa

5. When did Samuel establish Québec?
   - ○ 1608
   - ○ 1708
   - ○ 1808